A Little Bit of Life

Poems by Kathryn Browning

A CIP catalogue record for this book is available from the British Library.

ISBN 1-904169-02-3

© Copyright Kathryn Browning 2001

CLASSIFICATION: POETRY

This book is sold under the condition that it shall not, by way of trade or otherwise, be lent, resold, hired out or otherwise circulated without the publisher's prior consent in any form of binding or cover other than that in which it is published and without a similar condition including this condition being imposed on the subsequent purchaser.

Printed and bound in Great Britain.
First published in Great Britain in 2001 by
United Press Ltd
44a St James Street
Burnley
BB11 1NQ
Tel: 01282 459533
Fax: 01282 412679
All Rights Reserved

www.upltd.co.uk

CONTENTS

5	A Poets View
	Welcome
6	A Special Cat
7	Forbidden Love
8	It's Just A Day Case
9	Encouragement
	A Charity Shop
10	Thoughts On An Induction Programme
11	Secret Love
12	Holiday Alone
	Life Song
13	Stress
14	A Silent Enemy
15	A Receptionist
16	Tribute To The Healers
17	To A Favourite Chum
18	A Car Park Attendant
19	A Refugee
20	To Someone Special
21	Child Sitting
22	Teenage Holiday
	Another Bomb
23	In Love
24	Oh To Be A Volunteer
25	Pigeons
26	A Wedding Anniversary
	To Whom It May Concern
27	Pain
28	To The Mums
29	Grief
30	Goodbye Garden
31	It's Over

A POETS VIEW

When you write a poem and read it out loud, better by far a person alone, not a crowd
You look for reaction, its not always good, criticism taken seriously, as it should

Not everyone enjoys poetry, of this I am sure, rewards are all mine, when requested, some more.

WELCOME

"We have a wonderful addition, a baby", magic words
Please listen, have you heard,
Congratulations and cards delivered by each post
Saying "a dream come true" trying not to boast
Welcome, we are so happy baby dear, lucky little baby to have such a caring mum and dad,
celebrations such as these are sometimes sad,
Another mouth to feed, adding to financial strain
lonely parent and singles thinking, why is it all such a pain
When you welcome this precious new person
bear in mind those other births forced to learn a hard lesson.

A SPECIAL CAT

I wish I had a cat, no use I live in a flat
they enjoy gardens and chasing mice
staying in doors, unkind not right
Christmas came, presents galore, a box so heavy to be sure
Ripping it open and there inside, a very big surprise
A black cat door stop with green eyes, friendly features
almost real, no bother to look after, what a prize
He will sit by the door adding to my home
no fear of him ever wanting to roam
Thank you, I am so pleased, what a lovely thought
so much pleasure from a present newly bought.

FORBIDDEN LOVE

Firstly, its the all consuming and tingling feel I love
Energy and confidence abound, not needing a shove
Tolerance, sparkling and needing less to eat, radiantly
glowing, looking into a mirror, thinking I look a treat
Falling in love with the unavailable is forbidden,
control of actions and thoughts, almost impossible,
you are so driven,
It must end soon, but, not yet
getting our act together, then set
Nothing can come of this complex time, dreaming,
maybe, all will be fine
Never to let it happen again, deny all kisses at the start
Trouble with any solution, each party must agree the part.

IT'S JUST A DAY CASE

A minor operation swiftly over, just a day case
Relax, no problem, doesn't mean haste
arrive early morning, we are keen to start
smooth running is important, each has a part
Nurse settles you in with a positive smile
"is it my turn now", not for a while
All so busy dashing to and fro
Reminding you of the saying its all go
Nurses are there with confidence, they do it so well
worthwhile assistance, care and understanding, you can tell
Porter and trolley, "are you ready for off, alright" "yes"
a nervous cough
Before you know it, the day theatre looms
lots of blue clad people, it will be over soon
Back in the ward "please, have they changed their mind"
silly, its over and done with, lay down and unwind
Nurse tucks you in, tea and biscuits are on the way
doing their best to ease your stay
Thank you to the marvellous medical profession
sensible eating and exercise is the lesson.

ENCOURAGEMENT

A poem of encouragement, how can we possibly put ourselves
in your shoes?
Many say "We understand", we haven't a clue
Support, kind words when you are down, reassurance, knowing
someone will be around
Family and friends at the end of a telephone
never feel alone
Normality at times, a necessary life, takes away the toll of strife
Sorry is such a short word we all are, just want it heard.

A CHARITY SHOP

Charity shops are situated all over the place
filling empty shops, using the space
We need volunteers, each notice displays
a few hours would do, not, every day
Being a volunteer, sometimes gives moments to treasure
comfortable shops, away from bad weather
Have you any wedding dresses?, an unusual request
delighted to look around, and do our best
Dress, shoes, hat and flowers, all in white
careful help not wishing the customer to look a sight
A brushed nylon nightie with long sleeves?
its a honeymoon, not an Artic expedition says the customer as
she leaves
Clothes by the sackful arriving each week, sometimes to
look and say "What rubbish, its a cheek"
A lone figure bringing possesions and clothes, unable to speak
Shops will continue for years to come,
Volunteers are essential, why not try becoming one?.

THOUGHTS ON AN INDUCTION PROGRAMME

Success, you have the job, what's the next step?
Compulsory training sessions, which must be met
filled with dread, and on your mind
Will the tutors be helpful and kind?
Held at a college in the country, we'll send a map,
Driving a problem glancing at directions on your lap
Suddenly you are there, a new anxious employee
apprehensive, relax, wait and see
Classes of eight ladies and one man, files at the ready outlining the plan
The tutor came in and smiled, then looked around the room
The training is straightforward, we'll be starting very soon
Bonding is a social comfort, we did it very well
introductions and chat, uncertainty dispelled
The training team have been patient, experience plus skill,
Nine people confident to deal with anything,
even colleague feeling ill,
We have all become friends and had lots of fun
really quite sad as its nearly done
Three days of training have raced by
It was really great, we thank you, is our cry.

SECRET LOVE

Occasionally you wish to say "I love you", but that's against the
rule afraid even to confess when, up against the wall
When the chip are down, you will deny it
for both our sakes its dangerous to admit
Frequently said, unmentionable love, I will not get involved
it brings mega emotions, impossible to solve
But, there are moments when looking into each others eyes
are we reading the wrong signals, love does apply
Keeping your word to remain silent, no matter what
Please remember always, I care, because secretly I love you a
lot.

HOLIDAY ALONE

There are compensation of being on holiday on your own
away from everyone, mail and phone
Can be nothing personal, delight in the getaways,
a change from busy and stressful days
Train, plane or coach trips, new scenery, and company to meet
relaxed and happy on a double seat
Forward planning is a joy to me
new places to visit, so much to see
One or two say, strange off on your own, your choice?
surely you miss the sound of another voice
Hard to explain, just accept the fact
its only a short holiday, and I will come back.

IT'S OVER

Its over, dreaded words, hoping it is a mistake
after a long night, slow realisation, when awake,

Missing and still loving thoughts, invade your day
cannot bear to talk about it, but, aching to say

If only feelings were attached to a tap
turning it off immediately, and that's a fact

Enduring these solitary days, trying not to think of
fabulous times, desolation near the brink

There is no cure, its all part of living
suddenly an empty space, anxious to be giving

That left over love has nowhere to go,
reluctant to let anyone know,

Plenty of work, start going out, join a club, maybe go to church
unrest continues when remembering, for you heart not lurch.

STRESS

Stress, is it good for you? hesitate before you answer, please do,
some say, it makes adrenaline pump faster around your body,
making you feel good, small quantities, suppose it could
Eternal stress each and every day, relief in cigarettes, alcohol
and worse, expensive escapes damaging your purse
Thoughts and concerns keeping you awake, morning comes so
soon, too much to take
This is not an ideal situation, but then, nothing ever is,
compensations, I'm a whiz kid,
I'll do it for a few more years, must get on my feet
plenty of time later on, to ponder, sitting on a seat
Fair enough, a little stress, challenges are fine, sorting out a
mess
Give yourself moments to look and unwind
deserve the freedom, no excuse, this pleasure is mine.

A SILENT ENEMY

What the hell is going on, its beyond belief, thousands and thousands need relief
Foot and mouth, two words bringing fear and horror, families losing lively hoods, dreading tomorrow
Animals being slaughtered and then burned to ash, years of hard work and planning, over suddenly, no cash
An unseen monster attacking like a silent army, farmers, hauliers and business, no defence, it descends so calmly
Next its a flood in another part of the world, millions homeless and lost, starving, waters rising, terrified boys and girls
Burning homes, murder another atrocious scene, headless people rotting, what does it all mean?
If everyone knelt down and offered up a prayer, surely it would be answered, knowing you care
These terrible times for some will pass, majority will have monstrous dreams, that, will last
One day the news will be its all over at last, desperate days a thing of the past
Empty fields and barns, not an animal in sight, farmers will say, we have lost the war to a terrible might
to start again and dry the tears, getting it right, taking many years
So please, hear the prayers one and all, needing so much to answer our call.

A RECEPTIONIST

Your job as a receptionist, interesting or boring?

Do you need a lot of knowledge to use and store
Its a public job, perhaps a worry, vital to be calm
and not in a hurry
It is under rated in many ways
Once mastered likely to stay
Telephone and people requiring information, is it this or that?
once in a while longing to chat
When you next see an advertisement for a receptionist post
Apply, be surprised, its a job more interesting than most.

TRIBUTE TO THE HEALERS

Healing centres were a mystery to me
seen the odd TV programme and book to read
A friend said "We are going out, call for you on Wednesday
you need some inner strength, what is this about?
"Its a healing centre" she said, with a smile
no pressure, you will know in a while
We were greeted with a warm handshake, and requested to fill
up a card details of any illness or injury, simple questions,
nothing too hard
Meditations were next, soothing, making you feel good, a cup
of tea, time for a chat, sociable with laughter, cannot beat that
A lady healer says, "Now its your turn" simply relax, nothing to
learn
Sitting in comfort, feeling a warm glow, her hands moving gently, over any injuries soft and slow
The feeling of relief is strange to describe
But, pain and hurting does subside.

TO A FAVOURITE CHUM

A difficult poem to write, anxious to get it right
Do not let a small unimportant issue bring you strife, good
and bad things happen all our life
Everyone makes mistakes, often unaware, upsetting loved ones
and friends, of whom we care
Your respect through out, has been without doubt
The doors remains open wide, available for you to step inside
Guidance in this situations is needed, do you ring? or
leave it to him, difficult to cope being out on a limb,
Sex like food available all over the place, vital and
necessary to fill a space,
Take away, fast food, why, they are just fine, umpteen people
use them many times
Loving sex is another matter, drawbacks, out of reach, waiting
for that lively spark, quality, attraction, and skilled to teach
Thinking about idyllic hours and buzz
telling yourself, I think I'm in love.

A CAR PARK ATTENDANT

I'm in charge of a car park, not an easy job especially in the dark,
Car drivers arrive, I show them a space plenty say, not that one,
I wish to be nearer the place
The worst is when its raining
Spaces available no not there the waters' draining
I wear a smart uniform, a mac when wet
A look in the mirror, straighten the tie, all set
When you see an attendant standing in the rain
be kind and helpful, not a pain.

A REFUGEE

A refugee, its a shame, forgetting in time, well anyway we are not to blame
Some Governments will send tents and food,
they will be alright, lightening their mood
Thousands and thousands are driven from their homes and land
a sorry state, pathetic sad little bands
On backs of lorries, tractors and trucks, freezing cold, sitting in queues just stuck
Remember each morning comfortable in bed, planning for the day ahead never spent the night on a mountain top high without shelter, warmth or food, even to buy
They are unwanted stripped of dignity nowhere to go
sad faces, crying children, despair and dread on show
Uncanny feelings, where are the men, shot, tortured or prisoners trapped in some den
the TV and newspapers show pictures of dejected refugees
we will send a donation is our plea
This misery is not for a month or two
what can any of us really do
Pictures of their misery imprinted on our minds
leaders and politicians seemingly good, but unkind
Money and compassion will certainly assist
refugees will ponder why oh why were we missed.

TO SOMEONE SPECIAL

I missed him and missed him but, dare not say
He came to mind many moments of the day
At night when quiet, I thought even more
Of suppers, talk, and wonderful moments by the score
After my accident in that hospital bed,
His card close by with words unsaid,
Will he still want me inspite of all this?
I long to see him and feel his warm kiss
I wrote him a letter, he answered by phone,
Of course he missed me, I'm not alone,
He will visit within a few weeks
My happiness flowed, I could hardly speak,
I'm still the same person, just have a few scars,
I know I'll be walking and driving my car.
I know when I see him and the smile on his face
Everything, suddenly, will fit into place.

CHILD SITTING

I'm very good at child sitting, so I have been told, hoping to continue, until very old
Usually arrive early before the set time, children are pleading to see me, and, pour some wine
Olivia and Sara are keen on Blind Date, Sophie and Alice staying up late
We all gather round and out come the sweets, Maltesers are favourite they are such a treat
Time for bed, upstairs we go, clean your teeth, my they are slow
Please tell us some stories when we are in bed
about your childhood and the life you led
Some of the happy times you must have had, perhaps you will tell us
some bits of the bad
Were you bullied, and did you like sport, name of your teacher by whom you were taught
Story after story, its getting late long past your bedtime, look at these beds, they are a state
We will tidy up now, a kiss goodnight
To be with you all again, feels to me, just right.

TEENAGE HOLIDAY

Radio one, lyrics without rhyme or reason,
is this the silly season?
No, I'm on holiday with six teenage girls
reminders of how things were, was my life such a whirl?
Whilst washing up and listening to Classic FM, I realise the
peace is good for me, and, possibly them,
Hard to prove I have done this and that,
do they look and think, its just all old hat.

ANOTHER BOMB

A car bomb exploded in parts of the world today
Its an outrage, many will say
The TV news reduces to tears
People stunned by horrifying fear
We try to understand how everyone must feel
careful never to say, time will heal
Such revolting evil people planning a bomb
knowing full well before very long
Human misery and pain will be down to them,
We wonder, do they ever, now and then
think about their savage deed
how can they dismiss it, without heed
The only comfort we can offer is, one day they will die
Standing before God, explanations scorned
no matter how hard they try.

IN LOVE

Being in love, is nothing new
yearning for it to happen to you
Finally it arrives, not what it seems
living becomes an agonising dream
Heartache, waiting for that call, telling you "I miss you"
probably not all
Off your food, fitfull sleep, love songs fatal in this state
Are you alright? please say, I cannot stand the wait
Settling down, why it always does, reality creeps in
controlling the buzz
Infatuated and so intense, sometimes unable to hear common
sense
So fortunate to experience bitter sweet torment
ideally a door stays open, surely meant
Love may end, good or bad, relived, possibly, although sad

Never to encounter the love drug, deep inner fire and passion
Taking no risks, at times, regret and anguish
forlorn, a hard lesson

When you feel it open your arms wide
embrace and say, "I want you by my side".

OH TO BE A VOLUNTEER

Now I have retired, shall I be a volunteer
A big decision, which course to steer?
A charity shop, have they lots of messy clothes?
Or, a volunteer with a uniform, anxious to show
Working in a hospital seems a good idea,
Making tea & coffee, dishing out good cheer
Filing, reception work, or making the bed
assisting the clerical staff instead.
Driving the patients mobile hospital trolley
Five passengers at a time, in door job minus a brolley
Up and down the corridors in complete charge,
Stopping and starting, an interesting occupation by and large
On second thoughts, not for me
Interview next, enquiring, then wait and see

PIGEONS

Pigeons, they are not looked upon as doing a good turn
they multiply, mess all over, fed by people, who never learn

Many of them becoming so tame, sure, one or two given a name

One day I watched an old lady clutching a carrier bag full
of goodies, breakfast toast, unable to finish
thinking, its cold today, pigeons will be famished

She threw handfuls of food over the ground, suddenly dozens
of pigeons arriving making incredible sounds

The old lady laughed and sat down wearily on the seat
I wonder, are these the only live beings to day to meet

We know they are a nuisance but the pleasure they gave
to one old lady, walking away, turning around to
give them a wave.

A WEDDING ANNIVERSARY

Your wedding anniversary, another lucky contented year
Enjoying happy times and visits you hold so dear
Making good memories to carry you through
Good times and bad, love will overcome certainly true,
So raise a glass and drink to each other
many years to follow, problems solved, easy with a cuddle.

TO WHOM IT MAY CONCERN

What are we doing, we ask ourselves?
Miserable, uneasy, fed up, only fit to help
Told time and time again, what we do wrong,
Repeated noisy accusations, please peace come along
Is a relationship necessary? no not like this
Kindness, laughter and gentle ways often missed
Churned up inside with a lump in your throat
longing to run away and escape, leaving a note
Wishing to be well and happy for the rest of your days
situations become impossible in various ways
Admitting its on the way out, but do be sure
never to return when going through the door
Thinking this is it, fantastic from the start
recognise at least, an unbroken complete heart.

PAIN

There are many forms of hurting and pain
causes may be illness, agony over and over again

Family quarrels and misunderstandings, it such a shame
both sides adamant, we are not to blame

Maybe a brief love encounter, not too bad, a little sad

Other ways of hurting are to ignore, anguish and annoyance
making us sore

Bitter realisation at the end of an affair, cowardly action a telephone call to make you aware

Kindness is necessary, not brutal attack, impersonal messages, a question, are they coming back?

For some anger takes over inspite of failure and loss
strong enough somehow to say, in charge, the boss

Occasional moments provoke and stir, happy families and
friends, remainders of the past

Thankfully life goes on, this uncomfortable dilemma will not
last.

TO THE MUMS

Mum, a little word, meaning so many things
Anxious to get it right needing super energy and wings
Millions have been one, far and wide
Care for ourselves, allowing to slide
It a difficult job, we all admit
Professionals careful, not to omit
Tiredness, tears, and a small person bringing fears
Older mums do understand, and, want to take over and hold your hand
We know you can manage, its proved each day
Enjoy, you can do it, come what may.

GRIEF

Grief and pain, known by most, hurt is intense, some comfort in words by post

Married or partners for years, one has gone, to hear their voice, how you long

Buck up now life goes on, how can you, tearing you apart hearing that song

People mean well, its for your own good, to carry on as you know you should

Watching young and old people stricken by grief, is it harder when older, picking up the pieces appearing bolder,

Agonising feelings, am I out in the cold, how will I manage must possessions be sold?

Grief can hit us at any age, devasting consequences, decisions to be made

Death or breaking up gives time to think, no quick cure in any form of drink

Time passes, one day to admit, its getting better, managing to laugh and eat without feeling sick

No words can wave a magic wand, or, bring back a special bond
All we can do, is, from time to time say, I will always remember you.

GOODBYE GARDEN

Mowing the grass, how the sun shone
Soon it will be all over, and I will be gone
The flowers seem to smile at me
See how lovely we are, look and see
The hills and trees so beautiful, I catch my breath
Thought I would be here until my death,
New people will be coming, but, I will leave a bit of me in
every blade of grass, flower and tree,
Without my early morning stroll, so hard to bear
Nothing will ever, ever compare
Continue to grow and smile at the sun
I'll treasure my pictures, each and every one.

LIFE SONG

Listen to the song of life, as days go by
sometimes its loud, then soft, you wonder why?
Life is cruel to some over and over again
possibly someone, somewhere thinks, they can take the strain
To be brave and silent, courage is needed to see one through
whispering I can manage, not much to do
Notice should be taken of this silent band
pushed aside by the noisy, complaining and demanding
completely out of hand
Some days the life song makes you swell with pride
happiness it seems, far and wide
Suddenly the life song changes, chaos and upset, causing a din
as time passes, it is harder to say I will win
Survive on the happy times, future songs may be dark
eventually when the song goes silent, leave your mark.